WORKBOOK

Movie Studio Island

Aaron Jolly • José Luis Morales
Series Advisor: David Nunan

Series Consultants:
Hilda Martínez • Xóchitl Arvizu

Advisory Board:
Tim Budden • Tina Chen • Betty Deng
Dr. Nam-Joon Kang • Dr. Wonkey Lee
Wenxin Liang • Ann Mayeda
Wade O. Nichols • Jamie Zhang

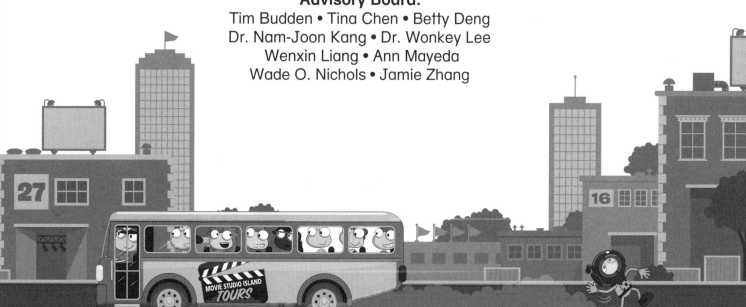

Pearson Education Limited
Edinburgh Gate
Harlow
Essex CM20 2JE
England
and Associated Companies throughout the world.

Our Discovery Island ™

www.ourdiscoveryisland.com

First published 2012
ISBN: 978-1-4479-0070-2

Set in Longman English 14/25pt
Printed in China (CTPS/01)

Based on the work of Anne Feunteun and Debbie Peters
Phonics syllabus and activities by Rachel Wilson

Illustrators: : Humberto Blanco (Sylvie Poggio Artists Agency), Anja Boretzki (Good Illustration), Chan Cho Fai,
Lee Cosgrove, Leo Cultura, Marek Jagucki, Mark Ruffle (The Organisation), and Yam Wai Lun

Contents

Welcome

1 **Write and match.**

1 She's 9. She has black hair.

She likes pink. Her name is

_____.

2 She's 11. She has red hair.

She likes movies. Her name is

_____.

3 He's 8. He has blond hair.

He likes skateboards. His name is

_____.

4 He's 8. He has red hair.

He has a sister. His name is

_____.

2 **Draw or stick a picture of yourself and a friend. Then write.**

My name is _____.

I am _____ years old.

I like _____.

My friend's name is _____.

_____ is _____ years old.

_____ likes _____.

4

3  **Listen and match.**

1
Matt

2
Simon

3
Carol

4
Kim

5
Ben

a

b

c

d

e

4  **Write.**

My favorite movie star is _____. _____ can

_____.

5 **Listen and write the numbers.**

a | 84 | | | | |

b | | | | | |

c | | | | | |

d | | | | | |

6 **Write.**

50	60	70
fifty		

80	90	100

7 **Write your favorite numbers.**

1   My favorite number between 1 and 10 is _____.

2   My favorite number between 10 and 50 is _____.

3   My favorite number 50 and 100 is _____.

Sing. (See Student Book page 10.)

8 Circle.

1 A gorilla is (shorter / taller) than a giraffe.

2 A hippo is (smaller / bigger) than a panda.

3 A mouse is (taller / smaller) than a rabbit.

4 A lion is (faster / shorter) than a horse.

5 A lion is (bigger / smaller) than rabbit.

9 Write.

Billy
12 years old

Andy
7 years old

Sue
9 years old

Darren
11 years old

Jane
10 years old

Christine
8 years old

1 (old / young)   Billy is _older than_____ Andy.

2 (old / young)   Darren is _____ Billy.

3 (smart / young)   Sue is _____ Christine.

4 (smart / young)   Jane is _____ Darren.

1 Free time

1 ✏️ **Match.**

chatting online

watching TV

reading the newspaper

skiing

playing the guitar

playing computer games

cooking

skateboarding

2 ✏️ **Write.**

1   He likes _____.

2   He doesn't like _____.

3   He _____.

4   He _____.

🔊 06 **Chant.** (See Student Book page 112.)

3  **Listen and write ✓ = like or ✗ = doesn't like.**

4 🖊 **Look at Activity 3 and write.**

1 What does Ruby like doing?

She likes _____ and _____.

She doesn't like _____ and _____

_____.

2 What does John like doing?

He likes _____ and _____.

He doesn't like _____ and _____.

5 🖊 **Write.**

What do you like doing?

I _____.

6 08 **Listen and write Y = Yes or N = No.**

7 **Look at Activity 6 and write.**

| painting   playing hockey   riding a scooter   walking the dog |

1 Does she like _____? _____, she _____.

2 Does he like _____? _____, he _____.

3 Do they like _____? _____, they _____.

4 Does he like _____? _____, he _____.

8 **Write about yourself.**

1 Do you like _____? _____, I _____.

2 Do you like _____?

3 Do you like _____?

4 Do you like _____?

9 **Listen and write ✓ or ✗.**

Me					
My mom					
My dad					

Fiona

10 **Look at Activity 9 and write.**

1 Does Fiona like playing computer games? _____

2 Does Fiona like watching TV? _____

3 What does Fiona's mom like doing? She likes _____.

   She also likes _____ and _____.

4 What does Fiona's dad like doing? He likes _____.

   He also likes _____ and _____.

11 **Write questions and answers.**

1  Does _____

_____

2  _____

_____

12 Number the pictures in order.

 **13** Write.

| eating | listening | looking | lying |
| sleeping | watching |

1 Ruby, John, Sam, and Jenny are _____ for Madley Kool.

2 The man in the studio says that Cleo likes _____ and

_____.

3 Cleo likes _____ in the sun.

4 Cleo likes _____ and looking and _____.

14 **What are Clara's goals? Listen and check (✓).**

15 **Look at Activity 14 and number.**

a Help people.

b Make new friends.

c Be a good student.

d Be a good son or daughter.

e Learn a sport.

f Learn to play an instrument.

16 **Write four goals.**

1 I want to _____.

2 I want to _____.

3 I want to _____.

4 I want to _____.

17 **12** **Read. Then write.**

This is Megan. She lives in a special house. It's a castle. It has 21 rooms and a big garden. She likes playing in the garden and likes reading outside. In the morning she can hear the swans, but at night it's very quiet. She doesn't like cleaning the castle—it's too big!

Name	
House	
Description	
Animals	
Likes	
Doesn't like	

18 **13** **Listen and check (✓).**

1

2

19 **Draw or stick a photo of a special house.**

20 **Read the words. Circle the pictures.**

| blow | cloud | shout | snow |

SOUNDS FUN!

ou   ow

21 (14) **Listen and connect the letters. Then write.**

1	b		ear	_____
2	ch		ay	_____
3	d		oy	_boy_
4	y		air	_____

22 (15) **Listen and write the words.**

1 ___out___   2 _____   3 _____   4 _____

23 (16) **Read aloud. Then listen and say.**

It's wintertime. The winds blow and black clouds are low. There is a lot of snow. Wear a coat, a hat, and a scarf when you go out.

24 Write.

Across →

Down ↓

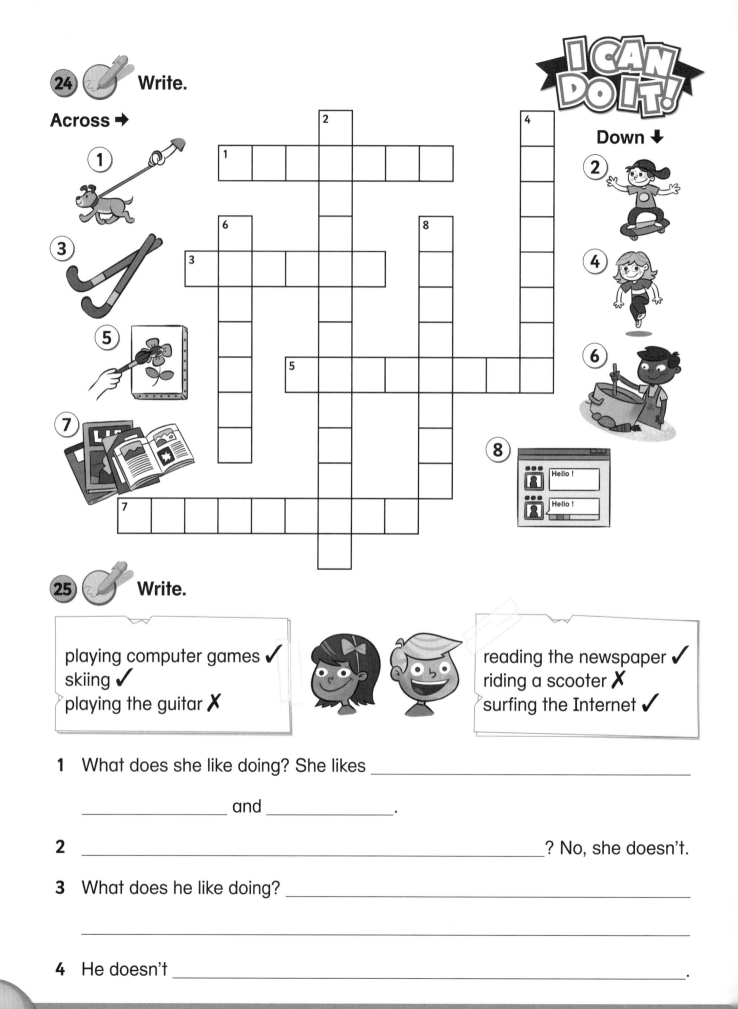

25 Write.

playing computer games ✓	reading the newspaper ✓
skiing ✓	riding a scooter ✗
playing the guitar ✗	surfing the Internet ✓

1 What does she like doing? She likes _____

_____ and _____ .

2 _____ ? No, she doesn't.

3 What does he like doing? _____

_____

4 He doesn't _____ .

26 What do or don't you like doing? Write ✓ or ✗.

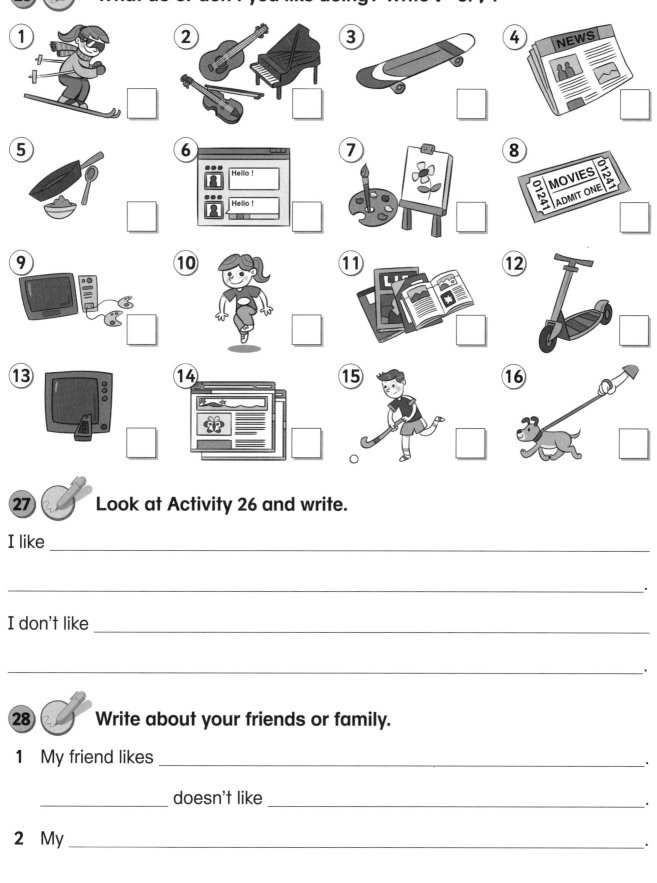

27 Look at Activity 26 and write.

I like _____

_____.

I don't like _____

_____.

28 Write about your friends or family.

1 My friend likes _____.

_____ doesn't like _____.

2 My _____.

_____.

2 Wild animals

1 🔊 17 Listen and number.

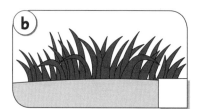

2 ✏️ Write.

crocodile   elephant   hippo   giraffe   lion   monkey

1   It's a lion.

2   _____

3   _____

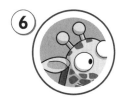

4   _____

5   _____

6   _____

18 **Chant.** (See Student Book page 112.)

3 What do the animals eat? Write.

| fruit   grass   insects   leaves   meat |

1 _____

2 _____

3 _____

4 Lions eat meat.

5 _____

6 _____

4 Write.

	Fruit	Leaves	Grass	Insects	Meat
Monkeys	✓	✗	✗	✓	✓
Lions	✗	✗	✗	✗	✓
Elephants	✓	✓	✓	✗	✗
Crocodiles	✗	✗	✗	✓	✓

1 Do monkeys eat fruit? _____

2 Do lions eat insects? _____

3 _____ elephants _____ fruit? _____

4 _____ crocodiles _____? _____

5 ✏️ **Match.**

① 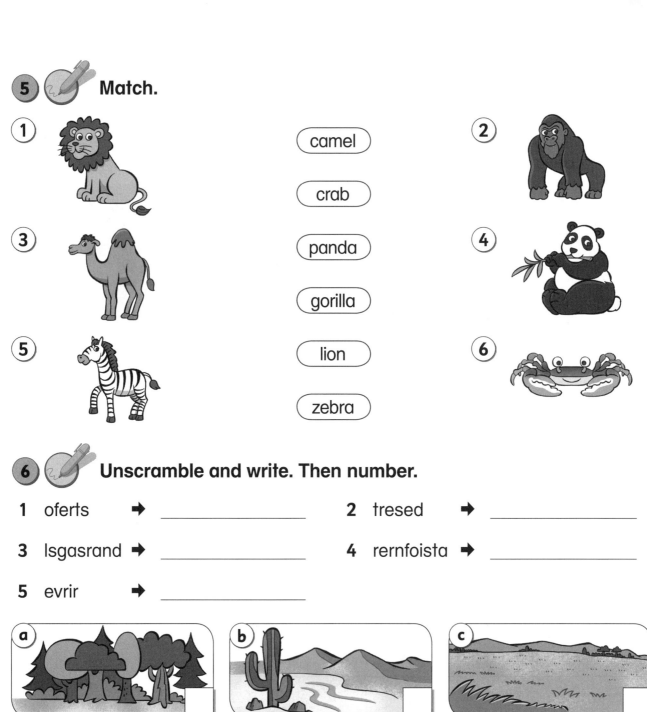 camel

crab

panda ②

③ gorilla ④

lion

⑤ zebra ⑥

6 ✏️ **Unscramble and write. Then number.**

1 oferts ➜ _____   **2** tresed ➜ _____

3 lsgasrand ➜ _____   **4** rernfoista ➜ _____

5 evrir ➜ _____

7 🔊19 **Listen and write.**

1 _____ live in _____ .

2 _____ live in _____ .

3 _____ live in _____ .

20 **Sing.** (See Student Book page 26.)

8  **Write.**

| big |
| drinking |
| lying |
| walk |

1 _____Camels_____ eat grass. They don't drink water much. They can run fast

and they can _____ all day.

2 _____ eat fruit and leaves. They like playing with their friends.

They are _____.

3 _____ eat grass and leaves of small trees. They like

_____ from the river. They have black and white stripes.

4 _____ eat worms. They like _____ in the mud.

They can't run very fast but they can swim.

9  **Look at Activity 8 and write.**

1 What do _____ eat? They eat _____.

Where do they live? They live in _____.

2 What do _____? They eat _____.

Where do _____? They live _____.

3 What _____? They _____.

Where _____? They _____.

4 _____ _____

_____ _____

10 Number the pictures in order.

a — "Oh, they eat grass ...."

b — "And where are the crocodiles?"

c — "Where are the hippos?"

d

e — "What do elephants eat?"

 11 Write.

1 Are elephants big? _____

2 What do elephants eat? _____

3 Do elephants eat cats? _____

4 Where are the crocodiles? _____ John's _____.

 12 Where do the animals live? Write.

forests   grasslands   rivers

1 Elephants live in _____ and _____.

2 _____ and _____.

3 _____

 **13** **Write.**

👍 Protect wildlife.

What are they doing to protect wildlife?

> He's joining a nature club.   He's learning more about wildlife.
> She's recycling.   She's getting her friends to help.
> She's giving money.   He's doing a school project.

_____

_____

_____

_____

_____

_____

_____

_____

_____

_____

_____

_____

 14 **Look at Activity 13 and choose two things you want to do. Write.**

I want to _____.

I want to _____.

15 **Write.**

1 Elephants live in grasslands and ____.

2 Elephants can ____ more than 300kg a day.

3 Elephants only have four ____.

4 Elephants don't eat ____.

5 Elephants can say ____ with their trunks.

6 Giraffes also live in ____ and forests.

7 Giraffes sometimes eat small ____.

8 Giraffes can live for one ____ without water.

9 Giraffes ____ standing up.

10 Giraffes have long ____ tongues.

16 **Find out about a wild animal. Write.**

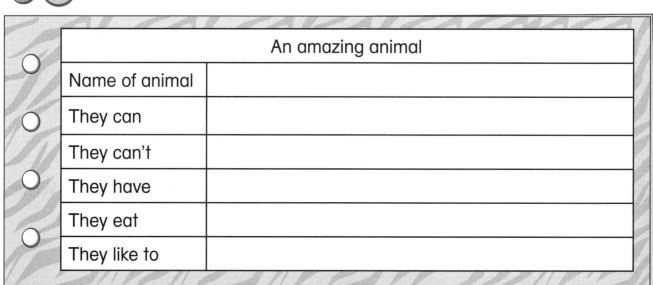

An amazing animal	
Name of animal	
They can	
They can't	
They have	
They eat	
They like to	

24

17 **Read the words. Circle the pictures.**

claw   draw   wall   yawn

SOUNDS FUN!

all   aw

18 (21) **Listen and connect the letters. Then write.**

1	th	i	n	er	_____
2	d	a	b	er	_____
3	s	u	nn	k	_____
4	c	ow	mm	oy	_____

19 (22) **Listen and write the words.**

1 _____   2 _____   3 _____   4 _____

20 (23) **Read aloud. Then listen and say.**

Welcome to the zoo. Look at the big cats! They have sharp teeth and sharp claws. I'm glad the wall is tall. You cats can't eat me for dinner!

21 **Write the animals' names. Then match.**

1

2

3

4

5

_____   _____   _____   _____   _____

6

a

9

_____

b

7

c

10

_____

_____

8

d

11

_____

e

_____

22 **Write.**

1 Do crocodiles eat fruit? _____ They eat meat.

Where do crocodiles live? _____

2 _____ They eat grass.

Where do zebras live? _____

23 **Draw or stick a photo of an animal. Then write.**

Grassland	River

_____ live in _____.

They eat _____.

They can _____.

They can't _____.

_____ live in _____.

They eat _____.

They can _____.

They can't _____.

Desert	Rain forest

_____

_____

_____

_____

_____

_____

3 The seasons

1 Match.

- humid
- lightning
- stormy
- thunder
- warm
- wet

TODAY

29°

27°

19°

N
W — E
S

KA-BOOM!

23°

2 Look at Activity 1 and write.

Good day, everybody. What's the weather like today? Here in the

north, it's ¹_____. The temperature is ²_____

degrees. Don't forget your hat!

Let's look at the east now. It's ³_____ today. The

temperature is ⁴_____.

Now, let's see the west. It's ⁵_____ today. It's cool.

The temperature is ⁶_____.

In the south the weather is ⁷_____. There's ⁸_____

and ⁹_____. It's ¹⁰_____.

3  **Listen and number.**

a   b   c   d   e   f

4  **Write.**

1 What's the weather like today?

There's _____ and

_____.

2 What's the weather like today?

It's _____.

3 What's the weather like today?

It's _____.

4 What's the weather like today?

It's _____.

5 What's the temperature today?

It's _____.

6 What's the temperature today?

It's _____.

5  **Write.**

| fall   spring   summer   winter |

1

2

3

4

It's _____.　　It's _____.　　It's _____.　　It's _____.

6 **Write.**

| go camping   go hiking   go snowboarding   go surfing |

_____　　_____

_____　　_____

7 **Look at Activity 6 and write.**

1 He goes _____snowboarding_____ in _____winter_____.

2 She _____ in _____.

3 He _____ in _____.

4 They _____ in _____.

26 **Sing.** (See Student Book page 38.)

8  Number.

1 She likes eating peaches in summer.

2 She goes to the park in winter.

3 She likes watching flowers grow in spring.

4 She likes flying her kite in fall.

9 Write.

Hi, Bill! It's warm at the beach. I love going water skiing in summer.

Hello, Jane! It's cold at the ski slope. I'm wearing my coat and beanie. I love going skiing in winter.

1 What's the weather like today?

_____

2 What's the temperature today?

_____

3 What does she do in summer?

_____

4 What's the weather like today?

_____

5 What's the temperature today?

_____

6 What does he do in winter?

_____

10 Write. Then number the pictures in order.

Action!   And I can sleep!   It's hot.
It's wet!   There's a beach.   We can climb!

_____   _____

_____

_____   _____   _____

11 Look at Activity 10 and write.

a Is he a farmer?   _____

b What's Sam doing?   _____

c Where are they?   _____

d Is it snowy?   _____

e Is it rainy?   _____

f What's Cleo doing?   _____

12  **Listen and number.**

👍 Be a good friend.

13 **Write three things a good friend does.**

Cheer your friends up.	Help your friends.
Lie to your friends.	Listen to your friends.
Make fun of your friends.	Talk badly about your friends.

1 _____

2 _____

3 _____

14 **Write about a friend.**

My best friend's name is Karen. We like playing computer games together. When Karen is sick or sad, I cheer her up. I give her a card. She likes cards.

_____

_____

_____

_____

15 Circle.

HURRICANE QUIZ

1 The center of the hurricane is
  a the heart. **b** the eye.

2 In the center of the hurricane
  a it's windy. **b** it isn't windy.

3 There are hurricanes in the
  a fall and summer.
  b winter and spring.

16 Write *hurricane*, *typhoon*, or *cyclone*.

Asia

China _____

Korea _____

North/Central America

Canada _____

Costa Rica _____

Australia

_____

South America

Mexico _____

17 Read the words. Circle the pictures.

chew fly new sky

SOUNDS FUN!

3

ew   y

18 **28** Listen and connect the letters. Then write.

1 | l | | oi | | k | _____

2 | c | | ea | | l | _____

3 | m | | ee | | f | _____

4 | w | | ai | | n | _____

19 **29** Listen and write the words.

1 _____   2 _____   3 _____   4 _____

20 **30** Read aloud. Then listen and say.

In my new jet I fly up and down, high and low. I see the clouds and the sun, the rain and the snow. I like to be up in the sky.

21 ✏️ **Write.**

Across ➡

1 It's rainy. It's 🌧️ .

3 It's hot and 😫 .

5 The ____ today is 18°.

7 18° means 18 ____ .

Down ⬇

2 I can hear 💥 KA-BOOM! .

4 I can see ⛈️ .

6 It's ☀️ . Let's go to the beach.

8 It's 🌩️ . We can't go to
   the beach.

22 ✏️ **Write.**

goes camping   go snowboarding   go water skiing   spring   summer   winter

Hi. It's ^{1}_____ here and it's really cold. I ^{2}_____

and go skiing with my friends. What's your favorite season? I don't like spring

because it's rainy, but my sister loves it. She ^{3}_____

in ^{4}_____ .

Hi. It's ^{5}_____ here and it's warm. I love the beach.

I ^{6}_____ in summer with my friends. It's my favorite season.

I don't really like fall because it's windy.

23 **Draw or stick a picture of your favorite season.**

24 **Write a letter to your friend about your favorite season.**

Hi, _____. It's _____ here and it's _____.

_____

_____

_____

_____

4 My week

1 **Match.**

(do karate)

(do gymnastics)

(have ballet lessons)

(have music lessons)

(learn to cook)

(learn to draw)

(practice the piano)

(practice the violin)

(study English)

(study math)

2 **Write.**

What do you do on Saturday?

| do | have | learn to |
| practice | study | |

1 I _____ gymnastics.

2 I _____ music lessons.

3 I _____ the piano.

4 I _____ karate.

5 I _____ the violin.

6 I _____ ballet lessons.

7 I _____ math.

8 I _____ cook.

9 I _____ English.

10 I _____ draw.

31 **Chant.** (See Student Book page 112.)

3 ✎ **Write.**

① 〔SAT. 7:00〕   ② 〔WED. 8:00〕   ③ 〔SUN. 5:00〕   ④ 〔MON. 4:00〕   ⑤ 〔SAT. 2:00〕

1 What does she do on Saturday?

 She has music lessons on Saturday.

2 What does he do on Wednesday?

 _____

3 _____ Sunday?

 _____

4 _____ Monday?

 _____

5 _____

 _____

4 ✎ **Look at Activity 3 and write.**

1 She has music lessons at 7 o'clock.

2 _____

3 _____

4 _____

5 _____

39

 **5** **Write.**

> afternoon   a quarter after 8   a quarter to 9   evening
> half past 3   midday   morning

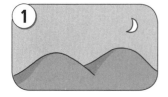

1 _____   **2** _____   **3** _____   **4** _____

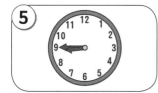
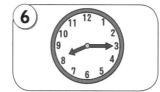
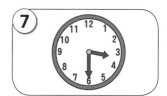

5 _____   **6** _____   **7** _____

6  **Listen and match.**

1

2

3

4

5

Sing. (See Student Book page 50.)

7 🔘₃₄ **Listen and draw the time. Then write.**

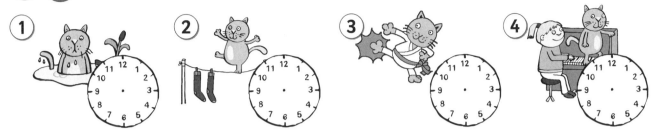

1 She goes swimming at _____.

2 She _____ at _____.

3 She _____ at _____.

4 _____

8 ✏️ **Write.**

When does she learn to cook?

She learns to cook <u>in the</u> _____

<u>morning</u>_____.

When does he _____?

_____

_____

_____

_____

_____

_____

9 **Number the pictures in order.**

a ... on Saturday.

b ... on Friday.

c But he can't swim.

d Where is Madley?

e ... on Monday.

 10 **Look at Activity 9 and write.**

1 What does Madley Kool do on Monday? _____

_____

2 When does he have singing lessons? _____

_____

3 When does he go swimming? _____

4 Can he swim? _____

 11 **Write.**

1 Does Madley Kool walk to work?

_____

2 Does he have a car?

_____ He goes

_____ by _____.

42

12  **Number.**

👍 Develop new interests.

a Write stories. ☐

b Learn a new language. ☐

c Get a new hobby. ☐

d Learn a new instrument. ☐

e Learn self-defense. ☐

f Learn about a topic. ☐

SUMMER ACTIVITIES

①

②

③

④

⑤

⑥

JOIN NOW!

13 35 **Listen and write.**

My name is Rosa. I think learning a new ¹ _____

is really fun. I want to learn the ² _____ this year.

Also, learning ³ _____ is great. I want to

learn ⁴ _____.

14 **Write about new things you want to try.**

My name is _____. I think _____

_____

_____

_____

15 (36) **Listen and write. Then number.**

① I ___walk___ to school.
Alex

② I go to school by _____.
Meiling

③ I go to school by _____.
Jodie

④ I go to school by _____.
Kabir

a

b

c 1

d

16 ✎ **How do you and your friends go to school? Check (✓) and write.**

		by car	by bus	by bike	by boat	by train	walk
1	Me						
2							
3							

1 I _____.

2 _____ goes _____.

3 _____.

17 Read the words. Circle the pictures.

glue   lie   pie   tie

18 37 Listen and connect the letters. Then write.

1   c   i   ke   _____

2   h   a   pe   _____

3   d   a   me   _____

4   sh   o   ve   _____

19 38 Listen and write the words.

1 _____   2 _____   3 _____   4 _____

20 39 Read aloud. Then listen and say.

Ha-ha-ha! The man with the tie has glue on his boots. He can't run. He is stuck with the pie in his hand.

21 **Listen, number, and check (✓).**

1

22 **What does Julie do on Saturday? Write.**

Julie's Schedule	
8:00 – 9:00	4÷2= 8÷4= 2×2= 3×7=
9:15 – 10:00	
11:00 – 12:00	
1:30 – 2:00	
2:45 – 3:30	
4:00 – 4:30	

She studies math at 8 o'clock.

23 Write one activity for each day and when.

SUN	MON	TUES	WED
Study math, afternoon			

THURS	FRI	SAT

24 Look at Activity 23. Write your own questions and answers.

1 When do you study math?

On Sunday I study math in the afternoon.

2 _____

On Wednesday _____.

3 _____

On Friday _____.

4 _____

On Saturday _____.

5 _____

On Tuesday _____.

6 _____

On Thursday _____.

5 Jobs

1 ✏️ **Write.**

┌─────────────────┐
│ a e i o u │
└─────────────────┘

1 f__r__f__ght__r

2 b__sk__tb__ll pl__y__r

3 b__ll__t d__nc__r

4 p__l__c__ __ffic__r

5 b__ __ld__r

6 mov__ __ st__r

7 __str__n__ __t

2 ✏️ **Write.**

1 I'm an _____

2 I'm a _____.

3 I'm a _____.

4 I'm a _____.

5 I'm a _____.

🎵 Chant. (See Student Book page 113.)

3 🔵 42 **Listen and number.**

a [hose with water] ☐   b [ballet shoes] ☐   c [handcuffs] ☐   d [basketball] ☐

e [tool belt] ☐   f [statue/award] ☐   g [astronaut] ☐

4 ✏️ **Look at Activity 3 and write.**

1 What does she want to be? <u>She wants to be a police officer.</u>

2 What does he want to be? _____

3 _____ does _____ want to be?

_____

4 What does _____?

_____

5 _____ want to be?

_____

6 _____

_____

7 _____

_____

49

5  Write.

athlete   carpenter   journalist   lawyer   mechanic
model   photographer   singer

_____ _____ _____ _____

_____ _____ _____ _____

6 Unscramble and write.

1 he / want / does / to / a / be / model (✗)

Does he want to be a

model?

No, he doesn't.

2 want / be / to / lawyer / does / a / she (✓)

_____

_____

3 a / do / want / be / to / you / photographer (✓)

_____

_____

4 singer / he / want / does / to / a / be (✗)

_____

_____

5

7 🎧 44 **Listen and write ✓ = want or ✗ = don't want.**

1 (a) (b)    2 (a)  COURT (b)

3 (a)  (b)    4 (a)  (b) POLICE

8 🖊 **Look at Activity 7 and write.**

1 He wants to be a _____. He doesn't want to be a _____.

2 She _____. She _____

_____.

3 _____

_____

4 _____

_____

9 🖊 **Write the questions. Then write your own answers.**

1  Do you _____? _____, I _____.

2 _____

_____

3 _____

_____

10  **Write.**

| acting   animals   dancing   jumping |

1

She loves _____

She wants to be a _____

_____ .

2

He _____ .

He _____

_____ .

3

_____

_____

_____

4

_____

_____

_____

11  **Write.**

What do you want to be?

_____

_____

52

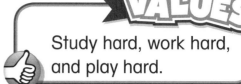

12 How much time do you spend studying? Write the number of hours.

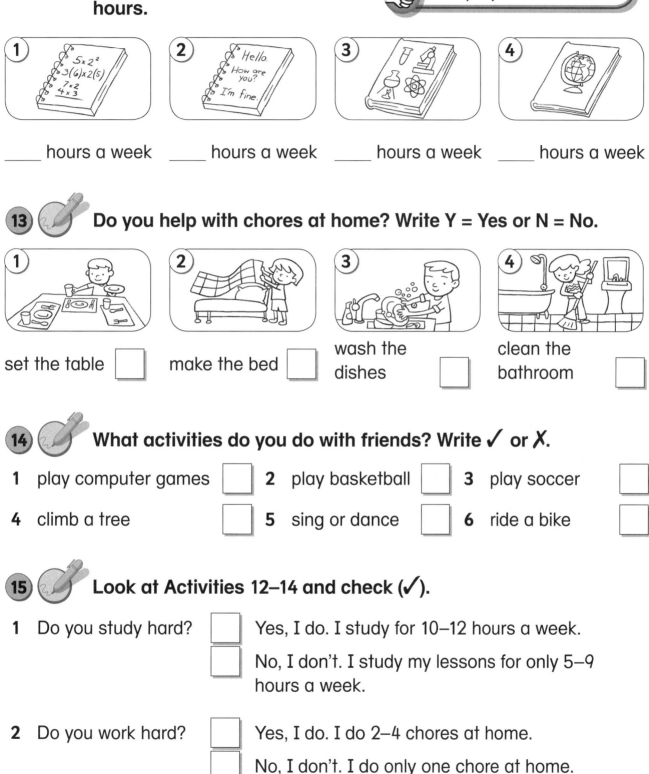

VALUES 5

Study hard, work hard, and play hard.

1 5×2^2 $3(6) \times 2(5)$ 7×2 4×3

2 Hello. How are you? I'm fine.

3

4

____ hours a week   ____ hours a week   ____ hours a week   ____ hours a week

13 Do you help with chores at home? Write Y = Yes or N = No.

1   **2**   **3**   **4**

set the table ☐   make the bed ☐   wash the dishes ☐   clean the bathroom ☐

14 What activities do you do with friends? Write ✓ or ✗.

1 play computer games ☐   **2** play basketball ☐   **3** play soccer ☐

4 climb a tree ☐   **5** sing or dance ☐   **6** ride a bike ☐

15 Look at Activities 12–14 and check (✓).

1 Do you study hard?   ☐ Yes, I do. I study for 10–12 hours a week.

☐ No, I don't. I study my lessons for only 5–9 hours a week.

2 Do you work hard?   ☐ Yes, I do. I do 2–4 chores at home.

☐ No, I don't. I do only one chore at home.

3 Do you play hard?   ☐ Yes, I do. I do at least 3 activities with friends.

☐ No, I don't. I don't spend any time with friends.

16 (45) **Listen and circle.**

1

Hello, Matthew. What do you want to be and why?

I want to be a (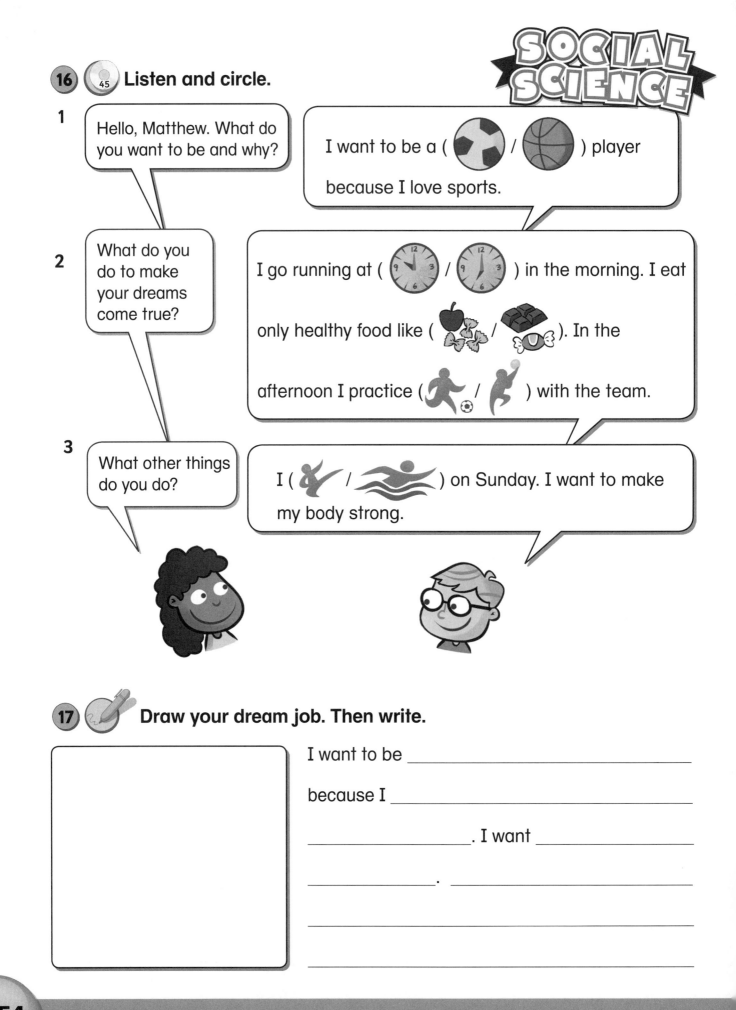 /) player because I love sports.

2

What do you do to make your dreams come true?

I go running at (/) in the morning. I eat only healthy food like (/). In the afternoon I practice (/) with the team.

3

What other things do you do?

I (/) on Sunday. I want to make my body strong.

17 **Draw your dream job. Then write.**

I want to be _____

because I _____

_____. I want _____

_____. _____

_____

54

18 Read the words. Circle the pictures.

jungle   paddle   rainy   sunny

SOUNDS FUN!

le   y

19 46 Listen and connect the letters. Then write.

1 | s | e | ll | ll | _____

2 | y | w | e | m | _____

3 | s | c | i | f | _____

4 | s | m | ar | ow | _____

20 47 Listen and write the words.

1 _____   2 _____   3 _____   4 _____

21 48 Read aloud. Then listen and say.

We paddle down the river in our boat. The jungle is loud and the sun is hot.
Look at that yellow snake! Look at that red and blue bird!

22 ✎ **Write the jobs.**

1 _____

2 _____

3 _____

4 _____

5 _____

6 _____

7 _____

8 _____

9 _____

10 _____

23 🔘49 **Listen, number, and check (✓). Then write.**

☐ a b

☐ a COURT b

☐ a b

☐ a b

1 _____ Yes, he does.

2 _____ No, she doesn't.

3 What does she want to be? _____

4 What does he want to be? _____

24 **Draw and write two things you want to be or don't want to be.**

✓

I can _____.

I like _____.

I want to be _____.

✗

I don't want to be _____.

6 In the rain forest

 1 **Match.**

(bridge) (hut) (mountain) (nest) (valley) (vines) (waterfall)

  2 **Write.**

across   between   and   near   over

 ①    ②    ③    ④

1 I'm swimming _____ the _____.

2 The bird is flying _____ the _____.

3 She's standing _____ the _____.

4 The _____ is _____ the lake _____

the trees.

3 ✏️ **Write.**

1   Where's the giraffe? It's _____.

2   _____ doctor? She's _____.

3   _____ bus? It's _____.

4   _____   _____

4 🔊 51 **Listen and number. Then write.**

Where are the _____?   _____

They're _____   _____

_____.   _____

_____   _____

_____   _____

_____   _____

5 **Unscramble and write. Then match.**

1 akle _____

2 eas _____

3 slihl _____

4 staco _____

5 stap _____

6 rowdat _____

7 orthhug _____

8 donuar _____

6 **Check (✓).**

1 They couldn't go toward the hills.

2 He could swim through the river.

3 She couldn't walk past the lake.

4 He could walk around the mountain.

52 **Sing.** (See Student Book page 74.)

7 (53) **Listen and number. Then write.**

Could she run past the lions?

_____

Could he swim through the lake?

_____

Could they go around hills?

_____

Could he walk toward the coast?

_____

8 (54) **Listen and write ✓ = could or ✗ = couldn't. Then write.**

1

2

3
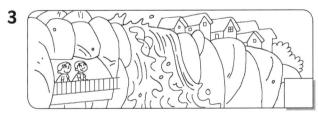

4

1 We _____ go by bus, but we _____ go by plane.

2 We _____ swim _____ the lake.

3 The huts are near _____ the _____.

4 We couldn't go near the lions but we _____ walk _____ them.

9 **Number the pictures in order.**

10 **Look at Activity 9 and write.**

a Who is wearing the tiger costume?　It's _____.

b Is Cleo on the building?　　　　　_____

c Where's the tiger?　　　　　　　It's _____ Ruby.

d Where's the spider?　　　　　　　_____

e Is the spider real?　　　　　　　_____

f Is Sam scared?　　　　　　　　　_____

g Is the snake real?　　　　　　　_____

11 **Choose a picture from Activity 9 and write.**

I like Picture A. She's wearing a tiger costume. She's very funny.

I like Picture _____. _____

_____

12 **Write.**

1

He's preparing for
basketball practice.
He needs:

- _____
- _____
- _____

2

She's preparing for
a school trip.
She needs:

- _____
- _____
- _____

3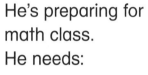

He's preparing for
math class.
He needs:

- _____
- _____
- _____

13 **Write five things you need for each trip.**

beanie   boots   bug spray   cap   cell phone   chocolate
compass   first aid kit   fishing pole   scarf   skis   ski jacket
sweatshirt   map   medicine   sandals   slippers   soccer ball
sunglasses   sunscreen   sweater   video game   water

A fishing trip	A skiing trip
1 _____	1 _____
2 _____	2 _____
3 _____	3 _____
4 _____	4 _____
5 _____	5 _____

14  **Write.**

> giant tarantula   hummingbird   parrot   tapir

1 I have a short neck. I live near the river. I eat bananas. What animal am I?

_____

2 I can fly. I have a long tail and colorful feathers. What animal am I?

_____

3 I can fly. I'm very small. I like flowers. What animal am I?

_____

4 I'm a big spider. I have long legs. I'm scary. What animal am I?

_____

15  **Write about your favorite rain forest animal.**

I like piranhas. They are a kind of fish. They have very sharp teeth. They live in the Amazon river. They eat meat, fruit, and seeds. I like them because they're scary.

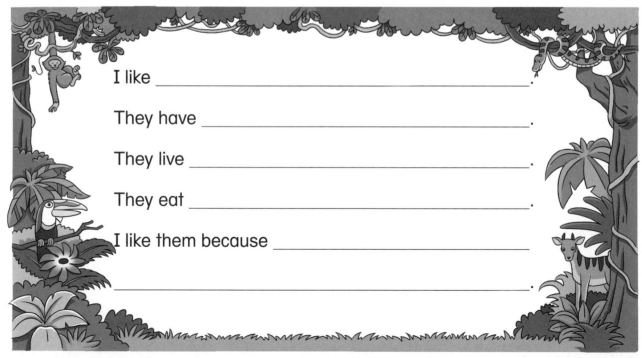

I like _____.

They have _____.

They live _____.

They eat _____.

I like them because _____

_____

16 Read the words. Circle the pictures.

ce ce ci cir

| circle | circus | ice | princess |

17 (55) Listen and connect the letters. Then write.

1	f	e	a	p	_____
2	g	l	tt	ss	_____
3	l	l	a	g	_____
4	s	l	ee	er	_____

18 (56) Listen and write the words.

1 _____   2 _____   3 _____   4 _____

19 (57) Read aloud. Then listen and say.

The princess is at home and the circus is here. It's a sunny day and the circus is funny, but the princess isn't happy. She wants to go to the city.

20  **Write.**

Across ➡

1 The boat is moving toward the 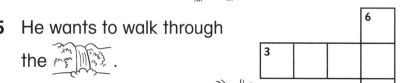 .

3 I want to swim in the 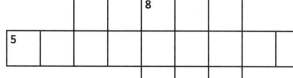 .

5 He wants to walk through
   the ⛰ .

7 The monkeys are on the 🐒 .

Down ⬇

2 A 🏠 looks like a house.

4 A ⛰ is taller than a hill.

6 A baby bird lives in a 🪹 .

8 People use a 🌉 to get from one side to the other.

21 (58) **Listen and check (✓).**

1

2

3

4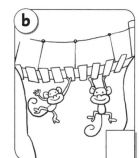

66

22 ✏️ **Write.**

1 _____ It's between the

elephants and the lions.

2 _____ They're near the hills.

3 Could you go past the lions? _____

4 Could you swim through the lake? _____

5 Could you swim through the river? _____

6 Could you walk around the lake? _____

7 Feelings

1  **Write.**

> blushing   crying   frowning   laughing   shaking
> shouting   smiling   yawning

1    He's _____.

2   She's _____.

3    She's _____.

4   He's _____.

5    He's _____.

6    He's _____.

7    She's _____.

8    She's _____.

2 **Draw the correct faces.**

1 The police officer is angry.
She's shouting.

2 The builder is tired.
He's yawning.

3 The movie star is scared.
She's crying.

4 The firefighter is happy.
He's smiling.

3  **Listen and number.**

4 **Write.**

1 he / shouting / angry

Why is he ___shouting___?

He's ___shouting___ because he's ___angry___.

2 you / yawning / tired

Why are you _____?

I'm _____ because I'm _____.

3 she / smiling / happy

_____

_____

4 he / shaking / sick

_____

_____

5 you / blushing / scared

_____

_____

6 she / crying / hurt

_____

_____

7 he / frowning / bored

_____

_____

8 you / laughing / excited

_____

_____

5  **Write.**

embarrassed   nervous   proud   relaxed   relieved   surprised   worried

1 _____   2 _____   3 _____

4 _____   5 _____   6 _____   7 _____

6 **Write.**

1 How do you feel?

I feel _____.

2 What's the matter?

I'm _____.

3 What's the matter?

4 How do you feel?

_____   _____

61 **Sing.** (See Student Book page 86.)

7 **Listen and check (✓).**

1 sad

2 nervous

3 worried

4 scared

8 **Look at Activity 7 and write.**

> being sick   crocodiles   flying   rainy days
> running   singing   snakes   swimming

1 What makes you feel sad? _____ make me feel _____.

2 What makes _____?

_____ makes me feel _____.

3 What _____?

_____ makes _____.

4 _____

_____ make _____.

9 **Write.**

What's the ¹ _____? Why are you ² _____? Are you sad?

No, ³ _____. ⁴ _____ because I'm worried. I failed my ⁵ _____.

 **10** **Write.**

STORY

angry   big animals   scared   worried

1 What makes her feel nervous?

_____

_____

2 Why is the shark frowning?

The _____

_____ it's _____.

3 What's the matter?

_____

4 How does the man feel?

_____

 11 **Write about great white sharks.**

Where do they live? How long are they? Do they have sharp teeth?

Great white sharks _____

_____

_____

 12 **Find out more about great white sharks. Then write.**

1 Colors: white and _____, _____ or _____

2 Food: _____, _____, _____

Help others in need.

13 Number.

1 Don't be embarrassed. I can help you study math at home.

2 It's OK. I can help you walk across the bridge.

3 Relax. Take it easy. You're very good at speaking.

4 Don't worry. I can help you find your mom.

14 What can you say to help? Write.

1
_____

_____

_____

2
_____

_____

_____

15 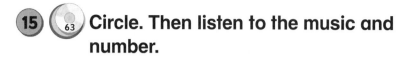 **Circle. Then listen to the music and number.**

a)

It makes me feel (scared / relaxed).

b)

I'm (crying / laughing) because it's funny.

c)

I feel (nervous / surprised) and happy.

d)

I'm (relieved / worried).

16 **Write the name of a song, singer, or band.**

1 What music makes you feel happy?

_____

2 What music makes you feel relaxed?

_____

3 What music makes you feel excited?

_____

4 What music makes you feel sad?

_____

17 Read the words. Circle the pictures.

| page | gem | gentleman | large |

18 Listen and connect the letters. Then write.

1	g	l	ee	n	_____
2	c	r	ou	n	_____
3	t	p	**oo**	n	_____
4	s	r	ai	d	_____

19 Listen and write the words.

1 _____   2 _____   3 _____   4 _____

20 Read aloud. Then listen and say.

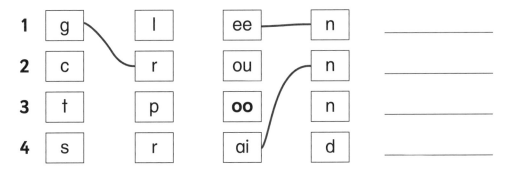

The gentleman looks at the gems. There are lots of small gems but he likes the large gem. How much is it? He asks. Now he sighs. The price is too high.

21  **Write.**

> frowning   laughing   nervous   relaxed   relieved
> scared   shouting   smiling

She's _____ because she's

_____ .

_____

_____

_____

_____

22  **Write.**

> angry   bored   embarrassed   excited   hurt   nervous
> proud   relaxed   sad   sick   tired   worried

crying	blushing	yawning	shaking
sad			

23  **Write.**

My name is Mario. In this picture, I am ¹_____ because I am

excited and ²_____. My basketball team is this year's champion.

Winning a game ³_____ feel ⁴_____.

24 **Draw or stick a picture of yourself. Then write.**

My name is _____. In this picture I am _____

_____

_____

_____

7

8 Action!

1 ✏️ **Match.**

1

2

3

- fishing
- horseback riding
- kayaking
- sailing
- snorkeling
- surfing

4

5

6

2 ✏️ **Unscramble the words. Then write.**

| farsorbud   file takecj   ginfshi loep   grinid stoob   norelsk   peldad |

1 Ruby is _____ fishing _____. She has a _ fishing pole _____.

2 John is wearing _____.

He is _____.

3 Jenny is sailing, but she isn't wearing a _____.

4 Cleo is kayaking, but she doesn't have a _____.

5 Sam is on a _____. He is surfing.

6 Madley Kool is wearing a _____. He's excited to go

_____.

3 (68) **Listen, number, and check (✓).**

	a	b		a	b
☐			☐		

	a	b		a	b
☐			☐		

4 ✎ **Write.**

1. Let's go horseback riding!

Great idea! I love _____.

2. _____

Sorry, I don't like _____.

3. _____

_____

4. _____

_____

Do _____ have _____?

Yes, I do.

79

5  **Write.**

bungee jumping   scuba diving   hang gliding   rafting   rock climbing

_____   _____   _____

_____   _____

6 **Write. Then listen and match.**

bored with   crazy about   fond of   scared of   terrified of

 ①   _____

 ②   _____

③   _____

④   _____

⑤   _____

Sing. (See Student Book page 98.)

7 Look at Activity 6 and write.

1 What is she _____? She's _____.

2 What _____? _____

3 _____ _____

4 _____ _____

5 _____ _____

8 Write.

A: The weather is nice! Let's go _____.

B: Sorry, I don't like sailing. I'm _____ it.

A: Oh! Well, let's go _____.

B: Great idea! I love _____.

A: Do you have a _____?

B: No, I don't! Ugh!

A: What do you want to do now?

B: Let's go _____.

A: Great idea! I love _____. I'm _____ it.

9 Write about yourself. Then draw or stick a picture.

What are you terrified of?	What are you _____?
I'm terrified of _____ _____.	I'm _____ _____.

10  **Number the pictures in order.**

11 **Write.**

| acting | good | making | movie star | scared of | sharks |

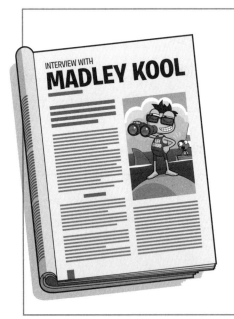

Madley Kool is a great ¹_____. He's
crazy about ²_____ adventure movies.
His new movie is *Great White Sharks*. In this
movie, there are some big ³_____.
Madley Kool is ⁴_____ sharks, but he's
a ⁵_____ actor. He says, "Sharks are
scary but I like ⁶_____."

12 **Write.**

1 What is Madley Kool crazy about? _____

_____

2 What is he scared of? _____

13 **Listen and write.**

👍 Enjoy all your activities.

> helping people   learning new things   making things
> playing sports   playing the piano   reading books

Maria

1 She's fond of _____.

2 She's excited about _____.

3 She's crazy about _____.

4 He's fond of _____.

5 He's excited about _____.

6 He's crazy about _____.

Bill

14 **Write ✓ or ✗.**

I enjoy activities that ….

☐	help me exercise	☐	start early in the morning
☐	help me get to know my family and friends	☐	teach languages
☐	help me make new friends	☐	teach math
☐	help me protect the environment	☐	teach science
☐	help me relax	☐	teach teamwork
☐	let me help animals	☐	teach music and the arts
☐	let me help people	☐	use computers

15 **Write two activities that you enjoy or don't enjoy doing.**

✓
1 _____
2 _____

✗
1 _____
2 _____

16  **Write.**

colorful   fish   hot   rain forests   sea   sea animals   white

1   Coral reefs are called the _____ of the sea.

2   There are a lot of _____ and _____ on coral reefs.

3   Coral reefs are _____.

4   Some coral reefs die when the _____ becomes too

   _____.

5   Dead coral reefs are _____ in color.

17  **Write.**

butterfly   butterfly fish   horse   lion   parrot   parrot fish sea snake   seahorse   snake   starfish

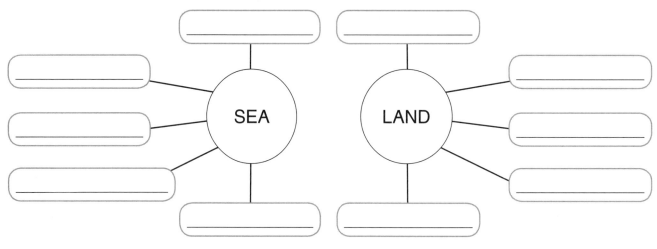

18  **Write.**

Why are most coral reefs found in hot seas?

_____

84

19 **Read the words. Circle the pictures.**

dolphin   phone   whale   whisper

SOUNDS FUN!

ph   wh

20 (72) **Listen and connect the letters. Then write.**

1	p	i	n	y	_____
2	b	u	nn	p	_____
3	t	u	m	le	_____
4	f	ai	ck	t	_____

21 (73) **Listen and write the words.**

1 _____   2 _____   3 _____   4 _____

22 (74) **Read aloud. Then listen and say.**

Look, the whale and the dolphin are on the phone! Here comes the shark. The fish are whispering. What's that on his head? Oh, it's a funny hat!

A: Let's go _____! Do you have a _____? **B:** No, I don't.	
A: Let's go _____! Do you have a _____? **B:** _____	
A: Let's _____! Do _____? **B:** _____	
A: _____ **B:** Great idea. I love _____ _____.	
A: _____ **B:** Sorry, _____ _____. I'm scared of it.	
A: I'm crazy about _____. **B:** I am, too. Let's _____!	

24 Write.

Hi, Gerry,

I'm having a great time here in the mountains. In the morning I go

1 _____. I'm fond of it. It makes me feel relaxed. In the

evening we go 2 _____. But I'm

3 _____ it. I don't like it very much. We are

going 4 _____ on Saturday. I'm

5 _____ it. It makes me feel proud that I can do it.

How's your vacation?

Raphael

25 Pretend you are on vacation at the beach. Write an email to a friend.

_____
_____
_____
_____
_____
_____
_____
_____

Goodbye

1  **Write.**

1 What's his name? _____

2 What _____? He likes making movies.

3 Why _____? He's smiling because he's happy.

2 (75) **Listen and circle.**

1	eating with Madley Kool	meeting Madley Kool	looking for Madley Kool
2	boys	girls	cats
3	a	b	c
4	a	b	c
5	a	b	c
6	a	b	c
7	relaxed	worried	nervous
8	three	four	five

3 ✎ **Write.**

1

Who is your favorite character in the story?

My favorite character is

_____.

2

What is your favorite chant about?

My favorite chant is about

_____.

3

What is your favorite song about?

_____

_____

4 ✎ **Think of your favorite movie star. Stick a picture of him/her in a scene from a movie.**

My favorite movie star is _____.

This scene is from the movie _____.

In this scene, he/she is _____. I like this scene because

it makes me feel _____.

5 **Read about Willie. Then write about yourself.**

My name is Willie. I'm 10 years old. I like playing the guitar and surfing the Internet in my free time. I don't like painting or drawing. My favorite wild animal is the gorilla. Gorillas live in the rain forest, and they eat leaves and fruit.

My name is _____

_____

_____

_____

6 **Write.**

Nov. 4, Sun.	Nov. 5, Mon.	Nov. 6, Tues.	Nov. 7, Wed.	Nov. 8, Thurs.	Nov. 9, Fri.	Nov. 10, Sat.
24°C	19°C	20°C	25°C	20°C	19°C	19°C

1 It's Tuesday. What's the weather like today?   It's _____.

2 It's Sunday. What's the temperature today?   It's _____.

3 It's Thursday. Is it humid?   _____, it _____.

4 It's Saturday. What's the weather like today?   There's _____

_____.

5 It's Wednesday. Is it stormy?   No, _____.

_____.

7 (77) **Read about Judy. Then write about yourself.**

My name is Judy. I'm 11 years old. I study hard every day.
I play basketball with my friends on Wednesday.
I learn to cook with my grandmother on Saturday. When
I grow up I want to be a lawyer or a journalist.

My name is _____

_____

_____

_____

8 (78) **Listen and write.**

1 What makes Amy feel …

   a proud? _Playing_ _____

   b nervous? _____

2 What's Amy …

   a fond of? _____

   b bored with? _____

9 **Write.**

1 What is a way of talking that is not the telephone? _____

2 What animal lives in rivers and only eats meat? _____

3 What weather has thunder and lightning? _____

4 What time is between morning and afternoon? _____

5 What do you call a person who takes photos? _____

6 What do you call the thing where baby birds live? _____

7 How do people feel if they do well at something? _____

8 What do you need to go kayaking? _____

Welcome

I'm taller than Sam/you/him/her.
He's/She's taller than Sam/you/me.
You're taller than Sam/me/him/her.
My hands are bigger.

Unit 1 Free time

What do you/they like doing?	I/We/They like skiing.
What does he/she like doing?	He/She likes skiing.
I/We/They don't like skiing.	
He/She doesn't like skiing.	

Do you/they like skipping?	Yes, I/they do.
	No, I/they don't.
Does he/she like skipping?	Yes, he/she does.
	No, he/she doesn't.

Unit 2 Wild animals

Giraffes eat leaves.		
Do giraffes eat	leaves?	Yes, they do.
	meat?	No, they don't.

What do crabs eat?	They eat worms.
Where do crabs live?	They live in rivers.

Unit 3 The seasons

What's the weather like today?	It's warm.
	There's lightning and thunder.
What's the temperature today?	It's 25 degrees.

I/We/They go camping in spring.
He/She goes camping in spring.

Unit 4 My week

What	do you	do on Saturday?	I have	music lessons on Saturday.
	does he/she		He/She has	music lessons at 2 o'clock.

When	do you	have music lessons?	I have music lessons	in the morning. at 2:15. at a quarter after 2.
	does he/she		He/She has music lessons	

Unit 5 Jobs

What	do you	want to be?	I want	to be	a builder. an astronaut.
	does he/she		He/She wants		

I don't	want to be	a builder. an astronaut.
He/She doesn't		

Do you	want to be a singer?	Yes, I do.
		No, I don't.
Does he/she		Yes, he/she does.
		No, he/she doesn't.

Unit 6 In the rain forest

Where's the hut?	It's	over the mountain.
		across the bridge.
Where are the huts?	They're	near the waterfall.
		between the mountain and the lake.

Could you walk around the lake?	Yes, I could.
	No, I couldn't.
I could walk around the lake, but I couldn't swim through it.	

Unit 7 Feelings

Why are you crying?	I'm crying because I'm sad.
Why is he/she crying?	He's/She's crying because he's/she's sad.

What's the matter?	I'm nervous.
How do you feel?	I feel nervous.
What makes you feel nervous?	Tests make me feel nervous.

Unit 8 Action!

Let's go	snorkeling!	Great idea! I love snorkeling.
	horseback riding!	Sorry, I don't like horseback riding.
Do you have	a snorkel?	Yes, I do. / No, I don't.
	riding boots?	

What are you fond of?	I'm fond of rafting.